MAKE IT!

Craft and Design 3-D

Anastasia Suen

Rourke
Educational Media

rourkeeducationalmedia.com

SUPPLIES TO COMPLETE ALL PROJECTS:

- 3-D printer
- air-dry clay in assorted colors
- aluminum foil
- candy (gumdrops or jelly beans)
- cardboard
- colored markers
- colored pencils
- computer
- cotton swabs
- glue stick or tape
- Lego base
- Lego bricks
- newspaper or cloth to cover your work area
- paper
- plastic filament spools
- plastic knife
- plastic mat or wax paper to cover your work area

- sandpaper
- scissors
- slicer software
- SD card
- .STL file (available free online)
- toothpicks or bamboo skewers
- tray
- X-Acto knife (for adult use only)
- yarn

Table of Contents

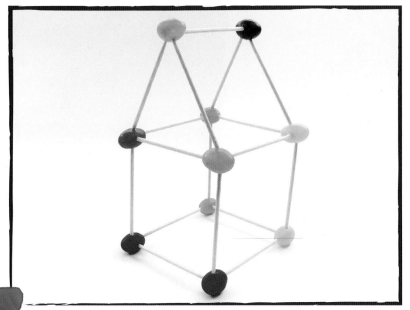

3-D Craft and Design

Explore the world of 3-D craft and design.

Write your name in 3-D. Design a clay creature and a candy house. Make 3-D art with foil and yarn. Discover how a 3-D printer turns a spool of plastic into a model you can hold.

Lego Letters

MAKE YOUR NAME THREE DIFFERENT WAYS.

Here's How: First, make a Lego name statue.

1. Write each letter of your name with Legos.

2. Build each letter so it stands up on the table.

3. Stand the letters next to each other.

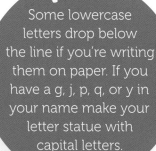

Tip: Some lowercase letters drop below the line if you're writing them on paper. If you have a g, j, p, q, or y in your name make your letter statue with capital letters.

Second, make a monogram.

4. Place new bricks next to each other on the table.

5. Move the bricks to make the first letter of your name.

6. Add another layer of bricks on top. Use different colors. Add special pieces.

Tip:

A **monogram** is the decorated first initial of someone's name.

Third, write your name on a Lego base.

7. Use a line of bricks to make the letters.

8. Write your name brick by brick across the base.

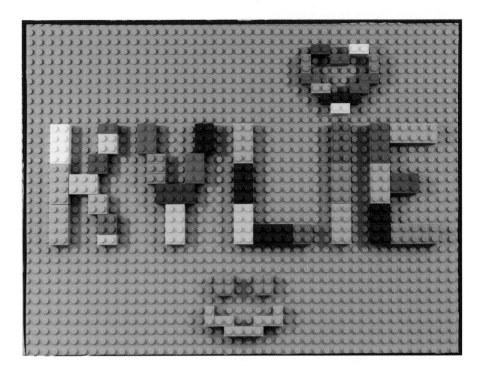

Is it 3-D?

How do you know that something is 3-D? Look for three **dimensions**.

1. Is it long? Can you measure the length from front to back?
2. Is it wide? Can you measure the width from side to side?
3. Is it tall? Can you measure the height from top to bottom?

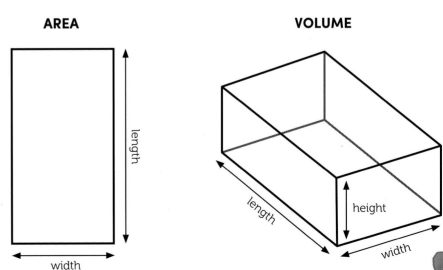

AREA

length

width

VOLUME

length

height

width

Embossed Foil Art

YOU WILL NEED:

- newspaper or cloth to cover your work area
- cardboard
- scissors
- glue
- yarn
- toothpick
- thick aluminum foil
- cotton swabs
- colored markers

MAKE ART WITH FOIL AND YARN.

Here's How:

1. Cut the cardboard into a rectangle or a square.

2. Cover one side of the cardboard with glue.

3. Put yarn on top of the glue. Make a design.

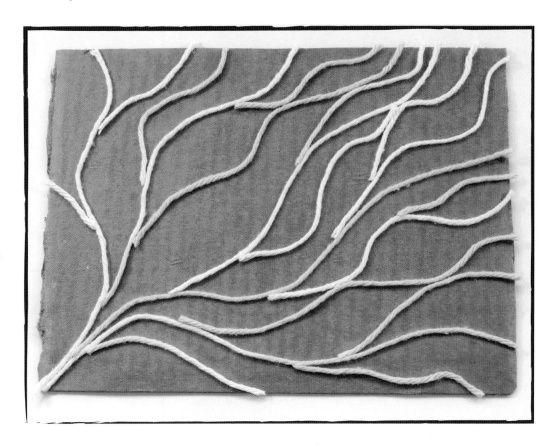

Is it 3-D?

To make an **embossed** design, you add something that rises above the surface. Gluing on the yarn adds height, making your design 3-D.

4. Measure the cardboard. Cut a sheet of foil that is larger.

5. Add more glue. Rub a glue stick on top of the cardboard and the yarn.

6. Place the shiny side of the foil on top of the new layer of glue.

7. Use a cotton swab to smooth out the foil.

8. Smooth out the foil from the center to each edge.

Tip:

Slowly and gently, rub the foil to make it stick to the glue. Carefully rub the foil around the yarn to emboss it.

9. Wrap each foil edge around the cardboard.

10. Color the spaces between the yarn lines. Use a different color in each space.

Silver Patterns

You can also use a dull pencil to make patterns in the spaces. After you make all of the patterns, rub black shoe polish over the foil. Count to ten, then wipe the polish off. Some black polish will stay in the pencil marks and show your 3-D patterns.

Clay Creatures

DESIGN A CLAY CREATURE.

Here's How:

1. Make a design with colored pencils and paper.

2. Draw a circle or an egg.

3. Then add a face.

4. Draw each item you add in a new color.

Is it 3-D?

Don't forget to design the back and the sides, too. You are making a **sculpture** in the round. When it is completed, it can be seen from all sides.

5. Warm up the clay with your hands.

6. Roll the clay into a ball or an egg.

7. Press it on the table to make the bottom flat.

8. Make the face.

9. Add your other items. Use a different color for each.

Tip:

Before you add the face, use a dull pencil to write your name and the date on the bottom of the clay.

Make An Action Scene

You can also make an action scene for your clay character. After you warm up the clay, create your scene inside a box lid or on a sheet of cardboard. Work from back to front.

Begin with the background. Use clay to show what is behind your character. Add layers of clay until you reach the front of the scene, where you show your character in action.

Is it 3-D?

A sculpture made of layers on a flat surface is called a **relief** sculpture. Artists around the world have created relief sculptures of action scenes for thousands of years.

Candy House

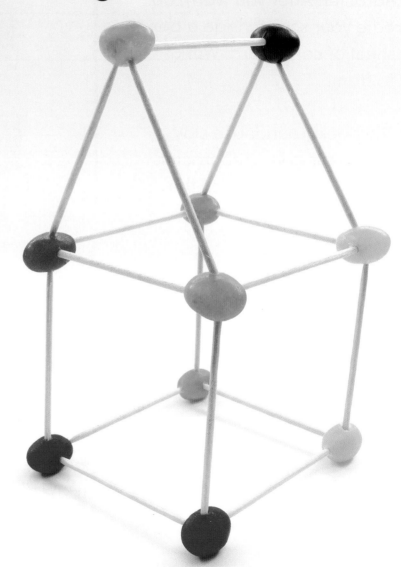

MAKE A HOUSE WITH CANDY.

Here's How:

1. Build the floor first. Make a square with four toothpicks.

2. Place a candy near each corner of the square.

3. Poke the toothpicks into the side of the candy.

4. Now you have a toothpick and candy square. The floor is done.

Tip:

Build the candy house on cardboard or a tray so you can move it when it is done. Place a sheet of wax paper on the tray as your work area.

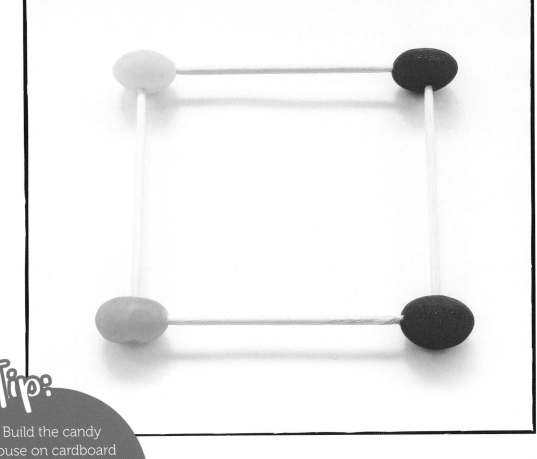

5. Build the walls next. Place a toothpick in the top of each candy.

6. Put a candy on top of one toothpick in the air.

7. Add a candy on the toothpick next to it.

8. Poke a toothpick into the side of each candy. Now one wall is done.

9. Repeat to build the other three walls. Now you have a cube.

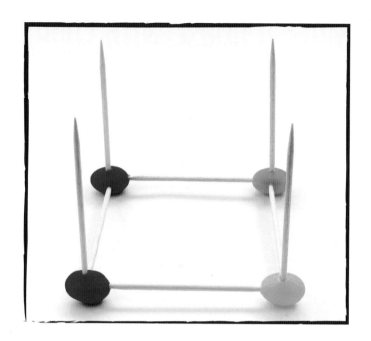

Tip:

To make a larger house, add another cube.

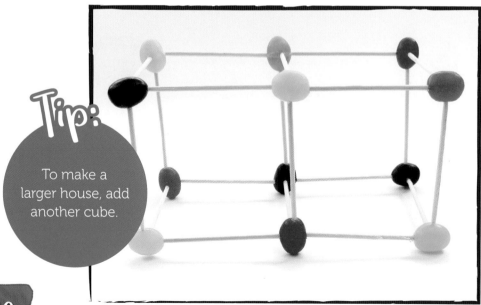

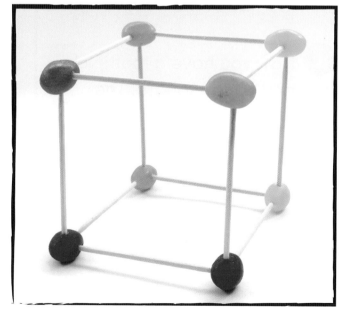

10. Add a roof. Make a toothpick and candy triangle on top of the cube. Begin above the wall on the left side.

11. Then make a triangle on top of the right side of the cube.

12. Connect the two triangles with a toothpick at the top.

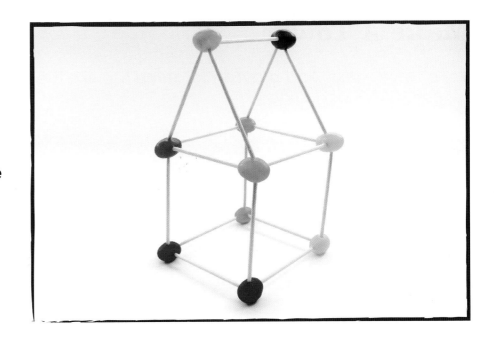

Tip:

If you made a larger house, add the roof to one cube at a time.

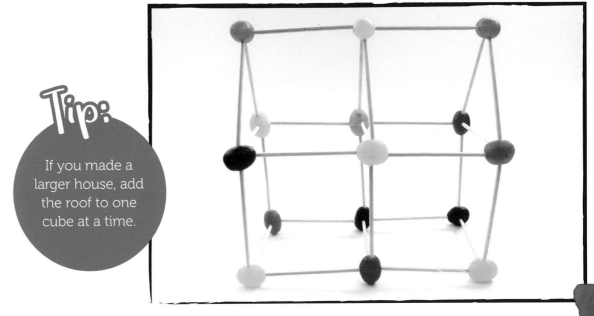

Make A Tower

Try a tower next. Add a pyramid at the top like the Washington Monument.

Is it 3-D?

An **obelisk**, like the Washington Monument, has three dimensions. It has length, width, and height. Just like a tower, an obelisk is wider at the bottom. A wide base keeps tall structures from falling over. If your tower falls over, make the base wider.

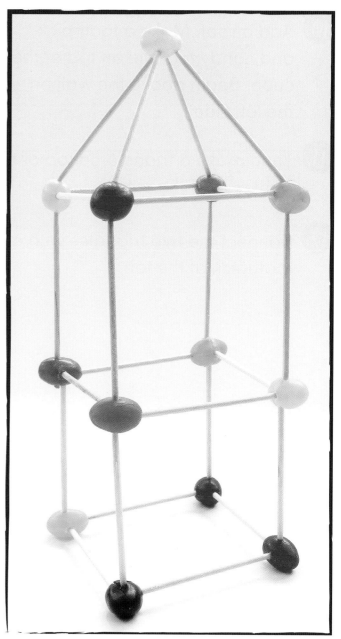

22

Print 3-D

YOU WILL NEED:

- computer

- .STL file (available free online)

- slicer software

- SD card

- glue stick or tape

- plastic filament spools

- 3-D printer

- sandpaper

- X-Acto knife (for adult use only)

Tip:

Many websites share free 3-D printer model files, called .STL files.

PRINT WITH A SPOOL OF PLASTIC.

Here's How:

1. Find a model you want to make.

2. Download the .STL file from a site such as https://pinshape.com.

3. Open the file with the slicer software. Make any changes you want.

4. Save the file on an SD card.

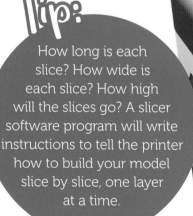

Tip: How long is each slice? How wide is each slice? How high will the slices go? A slicer software program will write instructions to tell the printer how to build your model slice by slice, one layer at a time.

5. Rub a glue stick on the plate. Add a thick layer of glue. Cover all of the plate.

Tip:

Some 3-D printer plates are covered with tape, not glue. Do not add glue to a plate covered with tape. The glue and the tape do the same thing. They both keep the hot plastic from sticking to the plate.

6. Choose a colored spool for your design. Ask an adult to help you load it.

7. Now the printer has to warm up. This is the pre-heating step. Ask an adult to do this for you.

Tip:

To melt the plastic filament and build your model, the printer has to heat up to 185 degrees Fahrenheit (85 degrees Celsius) or more. Always ask an adult to help you use the printer.

8. Take the SD card out of the computer. Place it in the printer.

9. Ask an adult to start the build.

10. After the printer warms up, the plastic will come out of the nozzle. Slice by slice, the printer will build your model.

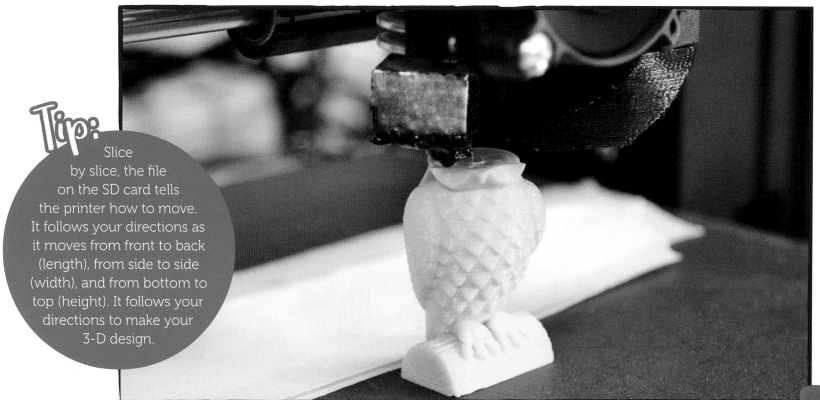

Tip: Slice by slice, the file on the SD card tells the printer how to move. It follows your directions as it moves from front to back (length), from side to side (width), and from bottom to top (height). It follows your directions to make your 3-D design.

11. When the printer is finished, it will be VERY HOT. Let it cool down. Let your model cool down, too. Then ask an adult to remove it from the printer.

12. Smooth out the edges with sandpaper. Remove any supports.

Tip:
The 3-D printer cannot print things hanging in the air. Your design must have supports for anything that extends out beyond the main body. After the model cools off, you can remove these supports.

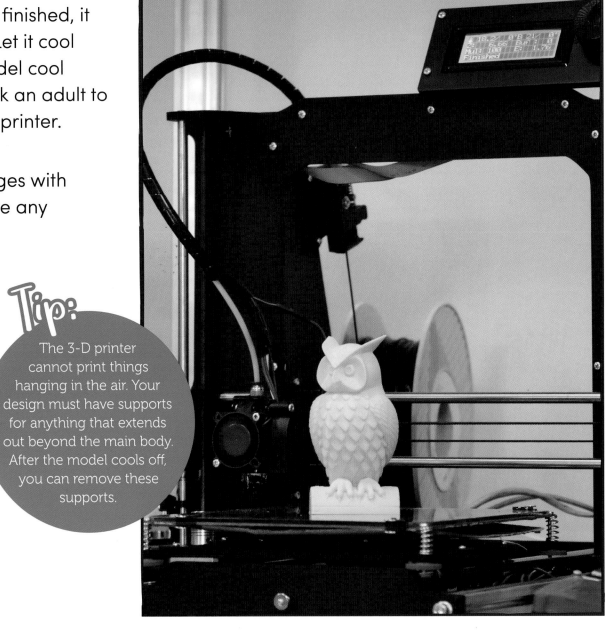

Why Does It Work?

The file in the SD card tells the printer how much plastic filament to use for each layer. The printer pulls the plastic into the extruder. The heater block makes the plastic hot. The printer nozzle pushes out a thin, hot plastic line. The printer follows the directions on the SD card as it moves the nozzle in three directions to make your 3-D model.

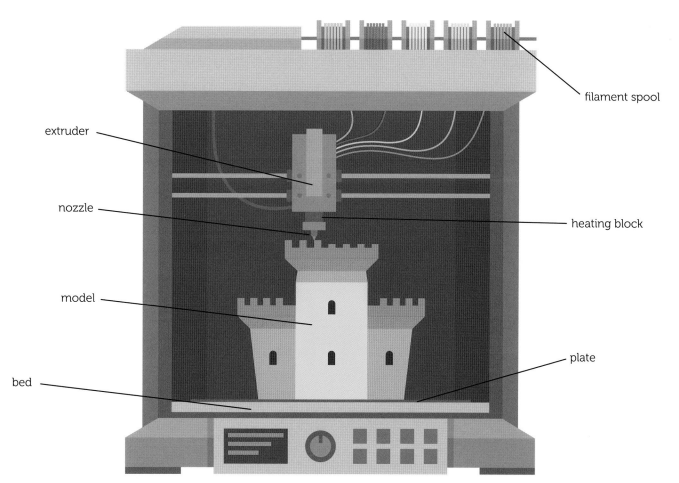

filament spool

extruder

nozzle

heating block

model

plate

bed

Glossary

dimensions (duh–MEN–shuhns): the three measurements of an object's size: length, width, and height

embossed (em-BOSSD): a raised design on paper or metal

monogram (MON-uh-gram): a decorated first initial of someone's name

obelisk (OB-uh-lisk): a tall stone with four sides that is wider at the bottom

relief (ri-LEEF): objects that are raised above a surface

sculpture (SKUHLP-chur): item carved or shaped out of clay

Index

Show What You Know

1. Explain the difference between 2-D and 3-D.

2. Why is the yarn glued to the cardboard before the foil?

3. Compare sculpture in the round and relief sculpture.

4. Did you build the candy house from top to bottom or from bottom to top?

5. After you download an .STL file, why do you need to use software before you put it into the printer?

Websites to Visit

www.cityxproject.com/toolkit

https://educators.brainpop.com/printable/3d-printable-moby

www.youmagine.com

About the Author

Anastasia Suen is the author of more than 250 books for young readers, including *Wired* (A Chicago Public Library Best of the Best Book) about how electricity flows from the power plant to your house. She reads, writes, and edits books in her studio in Northern California.

Meet The Author!
www.meetREMauthors.com

www.rourkeeducationalmedia.com

PHOTO CREDITS: Cover, Backcover, & Pages 4–22: © creativelytara; Backcover: © kyoshino; Page 4, 23, 24, 27, 28: © Marina_Skoropadskaya; Page 17: © molloykeith; Page 22: © JacobH; Page 24: © chaofann, pialhovik, scanrail; Page 25 © alex_ks, PangeaPics; Page 26: © kynny; Page 27: © bluebeat76; Page 29: © VOLYK IEVGENII

Edited by: Keli Sipperley
Cover and Interior design by: Tara Raymo • CreativelyTara • www.creativelytara.com

Library of Congress PCN Data

Craft and Design 3-D / Anastasia Suen
(Make It!)
ISBN 978-1-68342-380-5 (hard cover)
ISBN 978-1-68342-889-3 (soft cover)
ISBN 978-1-68342-546-5 (e-Book)
Library of Congress Control Number: 2017934541

Rourke Educational Media
Printed in the United States of America,
North Mankato, Minnesota